LIBERATION THROUGH HEARING

THE ART OF DYING

T0308138

LIBERATION THROUGH HEARING

THE ART OF DYING

by

TZE-SI HUANG

Illustrated by

DEMI

FONS VITAE

First published in 2018 by
Fons Vitae
49 Mockingbird Valley Drive
Louisville, KY 40207
http://www.fonsvitae.com
Email: fonsvitaeky@aol.com

Copyright by Tze-si Huang 2018

Illustrations by Demi

Library of Congress Control Number: 2018931753

ISBN 978-1941610-084

No part of this book may be reproduced in any form or by any means, electronic or mechanical, including photocopying, recording, or by any information storage and retrieval system, without permission in writing from the publisher. All rights reserved.

Dedicated to Venerable Tsokyni Rinpoche III
for his tireless efforts to transmit the precious Dharma.

Many thanks to Anne Ogden for her proofreading.

Printed in Canada

Contents

Contents, continued

THE INVOCATION PRAYER FOR ASSISTANCE AND PROTECTION

All Buddhas and Bodhisattvas, abiding in the ten directions,
Endowed with great compassion, endowed with foreknowledge,
Endowed with the divine eye, endowed with love,
Affording protection to sentient beings,
I bow my body, speech and mind.
Please condescend to accept my offerings.

XXX is now leaving this world,
Wandering aimlessly alone in the dangerous bardo path
Without relatives or friends.

He/she is confused, exhausted, and in great despair.

I beseech you to exert the power of compassion
And come to his/her rescue and escort him/her
Out of the dangerous bardo path
And point the way to the state of enlightenment.

INTRODUCTION

"Liberation Through Hearing" is the secret teaching revealed by the Great Guru Padmasambhava. It teaches how a dying person can be liberated and attain enlightenment in the process of dying. Even though it is the Buddhist tradition, the teaching is applicable universally.

Guru Padmasambhava was a great master of the Buddhist tantras and a yogi of immense power. According to legends, he was born from a lotus blossom about the same time as Shakyamuni Buddha. He was invited by King Trisongdetsen to establish the Buddhist teaching in Tibet. By pacifying and subduing the spirit world there, he transformed Tibet into a Buddhist land. He was the first Guru of the Nyngma school. He is more than a hero from the past. He is a present reality. He is constantly invoked by multitudes of Buddhist practitioners.

Anyone who is inspired or wishes to be liberated from the cycle of existence can apply the teaching. This book provides step by step applications of the teaching to achieve the great goal of ultimate liberation and enlightenment.

I - Life and Death

Life and death is a cyclical phenomenon.
It manifests that after death there will be rebirth.
After birth life inevitably leads to death.
Human consciousness is like a motor that triggers the beginning of a life.
It also causes the end of that life.
The phenomenon of life and death continues endlessly.
Everything that arises passes away.
But the essence of life exists eternally and without change.

II - Bardo

What is bardo?

Bardo is the period of a being in the intermediate state of existence between death and reincarnation.

This period can be divided into three stages:

1. First Stage - Preliminary
   It covers three and a half to four days.
   The primary Clear Light appears at the moment of death.

2. Second Stage - Reality
   It covers fourteen days.
   The secondary Clear Light appears immediately after death.

3. Third Stage - Becoming
   It covers thirty-five days. Starting from the eighteenth day, the karmic apparitions appear.

III - The Process of Death

Signs of approaching death

a. The five roots of deterioration - the eyes, ears, nose, tongue, and body.

(1) When the root of the eye begins to deteriorate, the dying person cannot see clearly. Also the light of the eyes disappears, and the eyeballs cannot move anymore.

(2) The dying person cannot hear anymore.

(3) The shape of the nose changes. It turns to the side, becomes twisted and is no longer straight.

(4) The dying person is no longer able to speak smoothly. The speech is slurred.

(5)The body of the dying person becomes dead heavy and difficult to move.

b. The disintegration of the vital elements: earth, water, fire, and wind.

(1) Skin, muscle, and bone belong to the earth. When the body of a dying person starts to disintegrate, it becomes very heavy and stiff like the earth. The dying person feels great pressure. This is the earth sinking into water.

(2) Blood, saliva, and all bodily fluids belong to water. At the time of disintegration, blood starts to coagulate and becomes frozen. The dying person feels cold and clammy. He/she feels as if he/she is being immersed in water, which gradually becomes feverishly hot. This is water sinking into fire.

(3) Temperature and bodily heat belongs to fire. At the time of disintegration, the dying person starts losing bodily heat and then turns cold. The dying person feels as if his/her body is being blown to atoms. This is fire sinking into air.

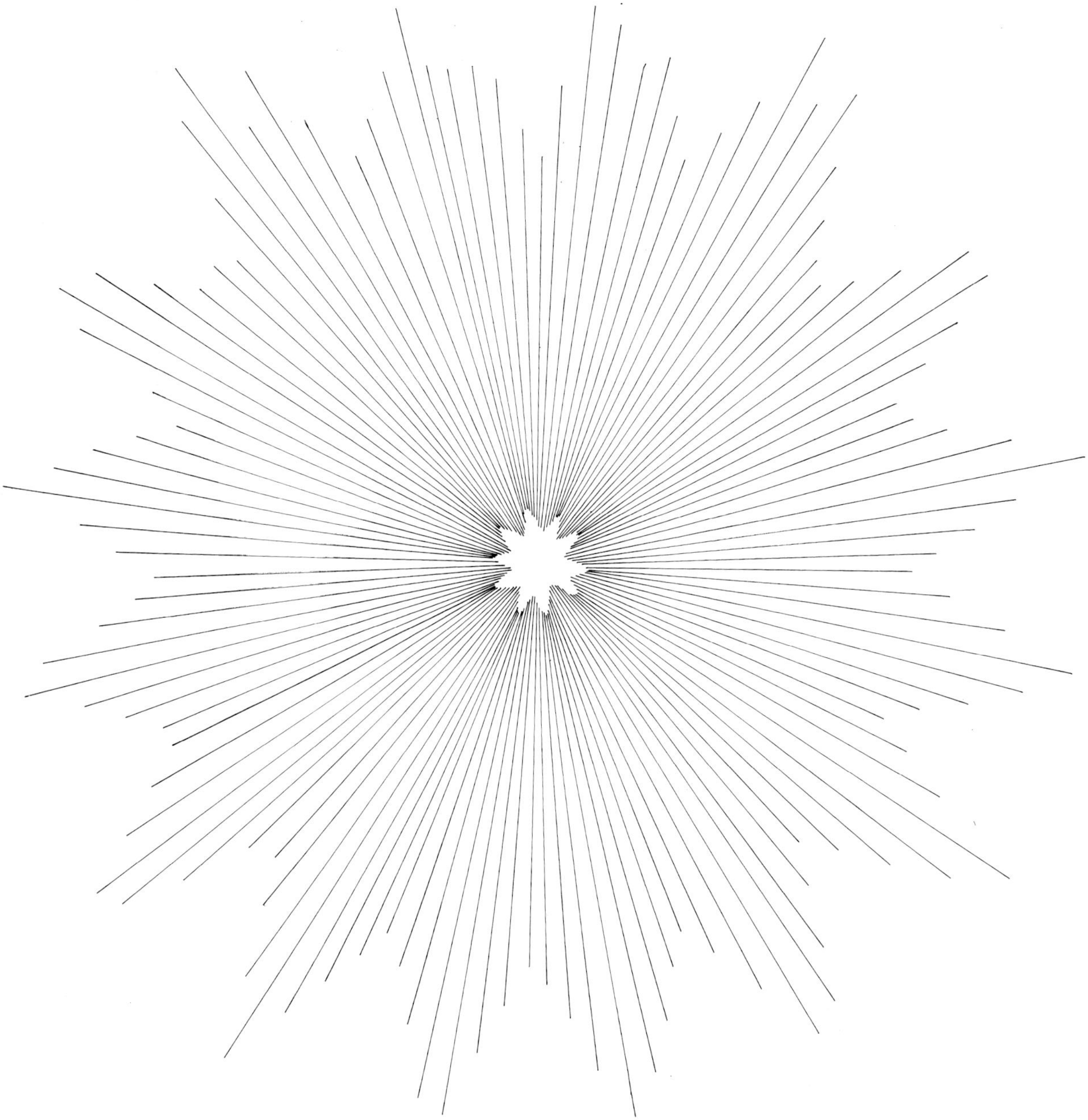

(4) Breathing belongs to the wind. When the wind disintegrates the dying person can only exhale and cannot inhale. Finally the mucous in the throat of the dying person blocks the windpipe and external breathing stops. The dying person feels a void and cloudless sky. This is air sinking into the bardo.

When these signs appear it is time to begin the process of salvation.

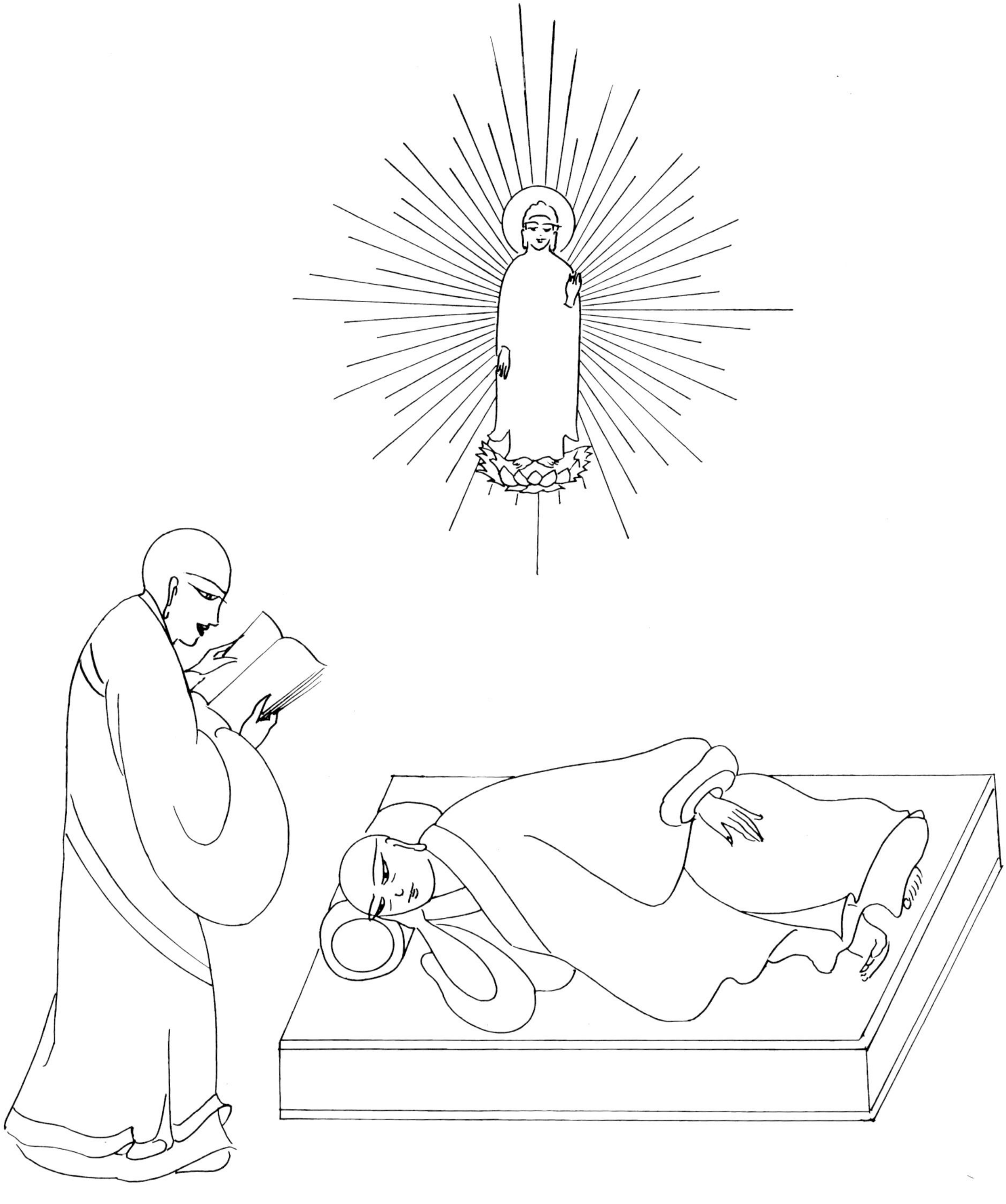

PREPARATION FOR THE CEREMONY

1. When the breath of the dying person is about to cease, turn the body to the right side (in the lion position) with the right ring finger pressed against the right nostril.

2. The conductor guides the ceremony. The best conductor is the root guru of the deceased. If he is not available, a spiritual brother or sister of the same faith will do. If they are not available, a spiritual friend will do. If a spiritual friend is not available, a trusted friend or somebody who is willing to help will do.

The conductor of the ceremony should undertake the task based on compassion purely for the benefits of the deceased without any motive for rewards of any kind.

The conductor should put his or her lips to the ear of the body without touching it. Then he or she should recite the instruction many times, distinctly and smoothly with proper intonation.

If there is no corpse, then the conductor should conduct the ceremony at the bed or the seat to which the deceased had been accustomed, summoning the spirit of the deceased to be present and listen to the instructions.

3. During the process no one should be allowed to weep or to wail. No slaughter of living creatures is permitted. The environment must be pure and silent.

4. Offerings: Arrange an altar with extensive offerings for the Buddhas and Bodhisattvas. If that is not possible, then offerings of lights, flowers, incense, tea and fruits will do. If that is not possible, then visualize the offerings.

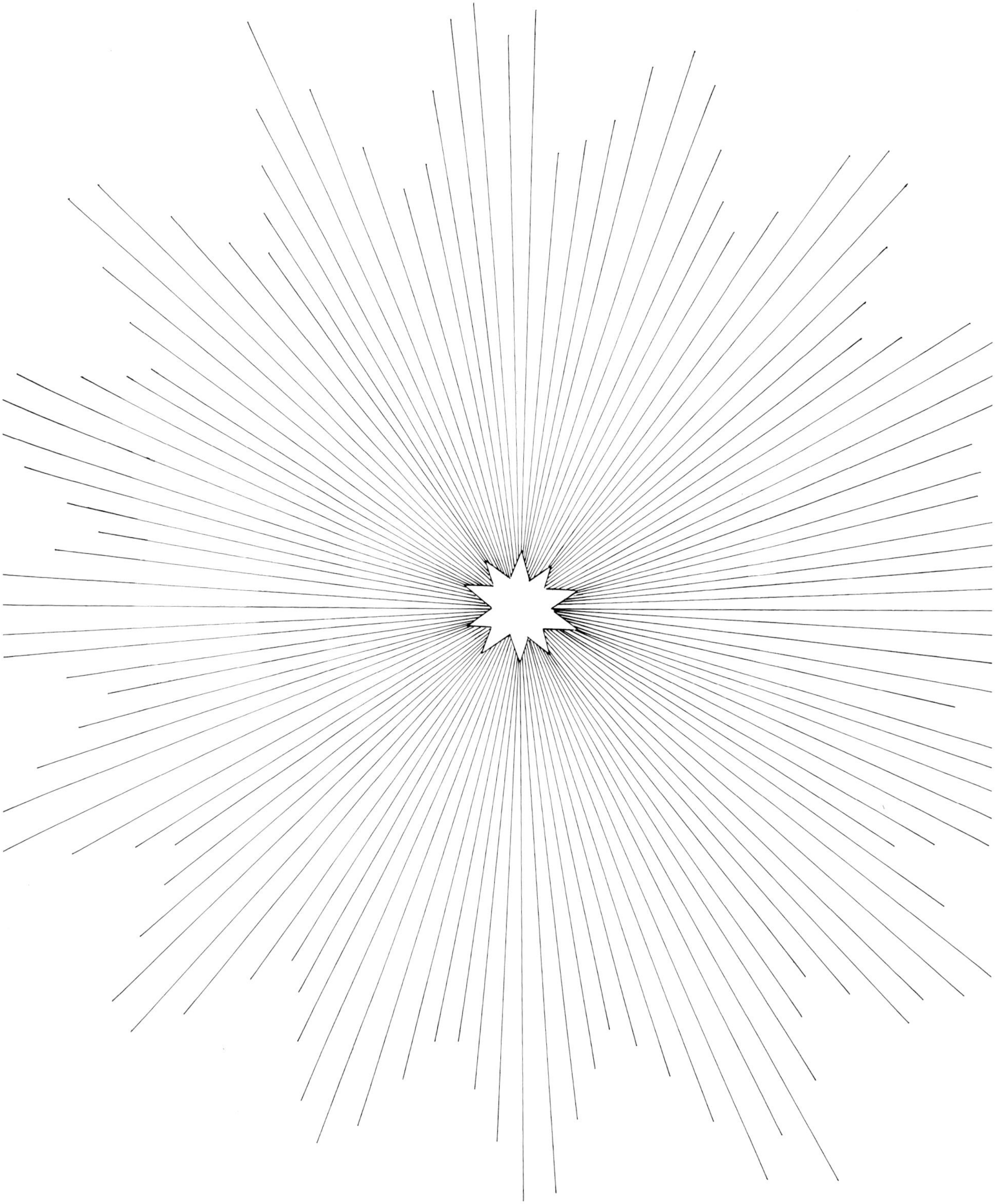

APPLICATION:
THE FIRST STAGE – PRELIMINARY

In this stage, the dying person's external breathing stops. The internal breathing continues. This stage lasts about three and a half to four days. After the last breath ceases, the blood and the final breath are absorbed into the central channel. The white radiant elements from the father move downwards. The red radiant elements from the mother move upwards. These two elements meet and merge into each other in the central channel at the center of the heart. The Clear Light from the primordial self of the deceased appears. It starts slowly, and then dimly. Finally it becomes so bright like the light of one million suns. Those who have high achievement in spiritual practice will attain liberation at death without outside assistance. There is no need to enter the bardo state. Some of the lesser or ordinary devotees may attain liberation when they hear the instruction. The rest are not able to see the light because they are still in the state of swoon. For them the instructions are necessary.

Ritual (Ceremony)

1. Arrange an altar with offerings for the Buddhas and Bodhisattvas.

2. Recite The Invocation Prayer three to seven times requesting blessings and protection from the dangers of the bardo.

3. Recite The Liberation Through Hearing Mantra seven or 21 or 108 times:

A BI JA DAN GA

4. When a yellowish liquid appears from the various apertures of the bodily organs, call the name of the dying person three to seven times, and recite this instruction many times:

"XXX, Listen very carefully.

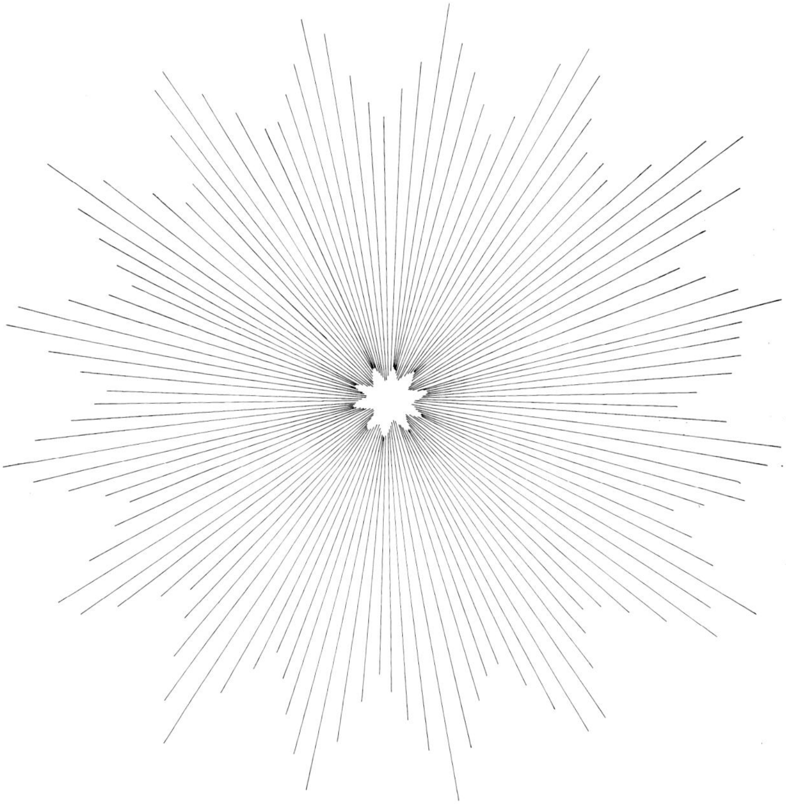

"Now the time of your death has come. You are not unique. It happens to everyone. You are about to experience the bardo state where all things are like the void and cloudless sky. At this moment know yourself and abide in that state. Please give up all your desires and attachments. Pray to the Buddhas and Bodhisattvas and protectors to beseech their assistance and protection. And meditate on love and compassion as well as enlightenment. Make a resolution for the benefit of all living beings that you will recognize The Clear Light and attain perfect enlightenment. Also, remember the following words at all times:

> "Whatever appears, no matter how tempting, terrifying or violent, I will recognize it as the reflection of my inner mind. Nothing is to be feared.

"Now The Clear Light is arising. It is the radiance of your primordial mind. Recognize it, retain it, and melt into it. You will be liberated."

THE SECOND STAGE – REALITY

After four days the deceased wakes up from the state of swoon. At this time, the deceased's senses of seeing and hearing etc. will be nine times stronger than those of ordinary living beings. Also, without a physical body, the deceased can move swiftly without any barriers. During this period, The Clear Light appears multiple times. This period lasts fourteen days. During the first seven days Buddha Deities will appear in peaceful forms. During the second period of seven days (days eight through fourteen), the same Buddha Deities will appear in wrathful forms.

PHASE I

During the first seven days the various peaceful Buddha forms manifest to help the dying person to attain liberation. Each day provides opportunities for attaining liberation and most people will succeed in one of these seven days.

The First Day

1. First arrange an altar with offerings for the Buddhas and Bodhisattvas.

2. Recite three to seven times The Invocation Prayer requesting blessings for their assistance and protection from the dangers of the bardo.

3. Recite The Liberation Through Hearing Mantra seven or 21 or 108 times:

A BI JA DAN GA

4. Call the name of the dying person three to seven times, and recite the instruction many times.

"XXX, Listen very carefully.

"Having woken up from the state of unconsciousness during the last four days, now you are in the second stage of bardo. You can see that the whole space is deep blue.

"The Buddha Variochana, white in color, from the Central realm comes to receive you. He sits on a lion throne, bearing an eight-spoked wheel in his hand and embracing his consort, Lady of the Space. From the heart of Buddha Variochana and his consort, the intensely dazzling radiant and clear blue light will shine directly upon your heart. The light is so bright that you will hardly be able to look at it. At the same time a soft white light from the deva realm also shines forth upon you. Due to the influence of negative karma, you will be terrified by the dazzling blue light and feel that you would like to flee from it. Instead you will feel drawn towards the soft white light. At this critical time, you must not be frightened by

the dazzling divine light. It is the light of Buddha Variochana's compassion and the light of wisdom.

"Ignore the soft white light. Don't even look at it. If you follow it you will be born into the deva realm and then be bonded by the cycle of reincarnations.

"Now trust in and devote yourself to the divine blue light of Buddha Variochana and the Lady of Space, and pray whole-heartedly:

> "Due to the influence of ignorance I wander through the cycle of reincarnation. May Buddha Variochana lead the way, the Lady of Space guard me from behind and escort me through the dangerous narrow path of the bardo, and lead me to the state of perfect enlightenment.

"Then melt into the divine dazzling light. You will transcend the cycle of reincarnation and attain liberation."

The Second Day

1. First arrange an altar with offerings for the Buddhas and Bodhisattvas.

2. Recite three to seven times The Invocation Prayer requesting blessings for their assistance and protection from the dangers of the bardo.

3. Recite The Liberation Through Hearing Mantra seven or 21 or 108 times:

A BI JA DAN GA

4. Call the name of the dying person three to seven times, and recite the instruction many times.

"XXX, Listen very carefully.

"The Buddha Vajra-Sattva appears from the East. He is blue in color and holds in his hand a five-pronged Vajra. He sits on an elephant throne, and embraces his consort, the mother of Mamaki, and is accompanied by two Bodhisattvas as well as attendant deities.

"A bright dazzling radiant white light emits from the heart the Buddha of Vajra-Sattva to you. It is so bright that you can hardly bear to look at it. At the same time a dull smoke-colored light from Hell also shines upon you. Due to the influence of anger you will be frightened by the brilliant white light. Instead, you will feel more comfortable with the dull smoke-colored light from Hell. Ignore it. Don't even look at it. If you follow it you will fall into the Hell realm and suffer unbearable miseries without end.

"Don't be intimidated by the brilliant white light which is the light of grace of Buddha Vajra-Sattva as well as the light of mirror-like wisdom. Believe whole-heartedly in the dazzling bright white light and pray as follows:

> "Due to the influence of anger and hatred I wander through the cycle of reincarnation.
> May Buddha Vajra-Sattva lead the way, Mother of Mamaki guard me from behind,
> Escort me through the dangerous narrow path of the bardo
> And lead me to the state of perfect enlightenment.

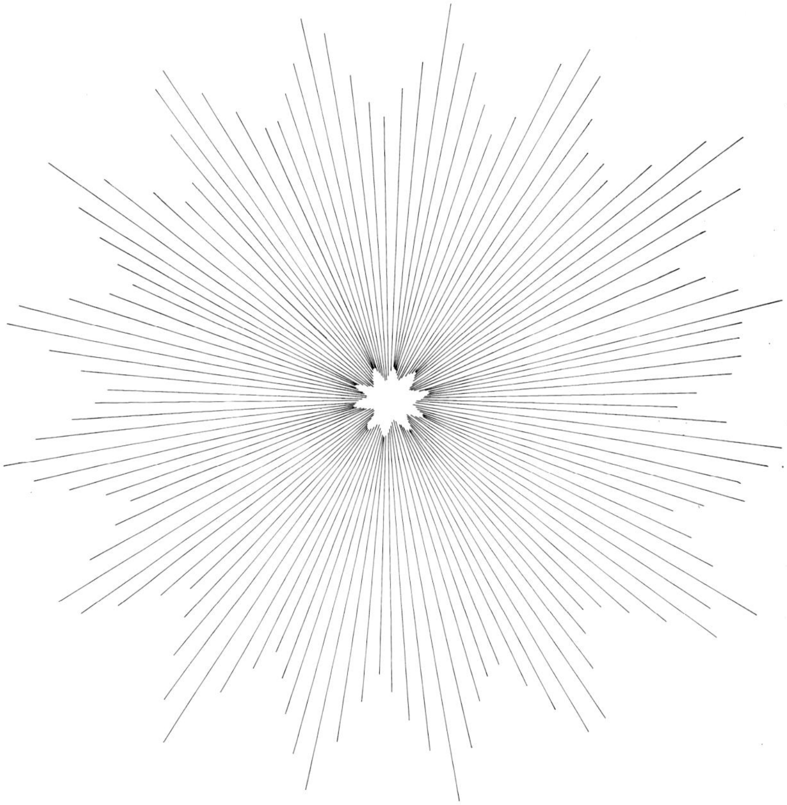

"Now with intense faith, melt yourself into the rainbow light in the heart of Buddha Vajra-Sattva. You will attain liberation instantly."

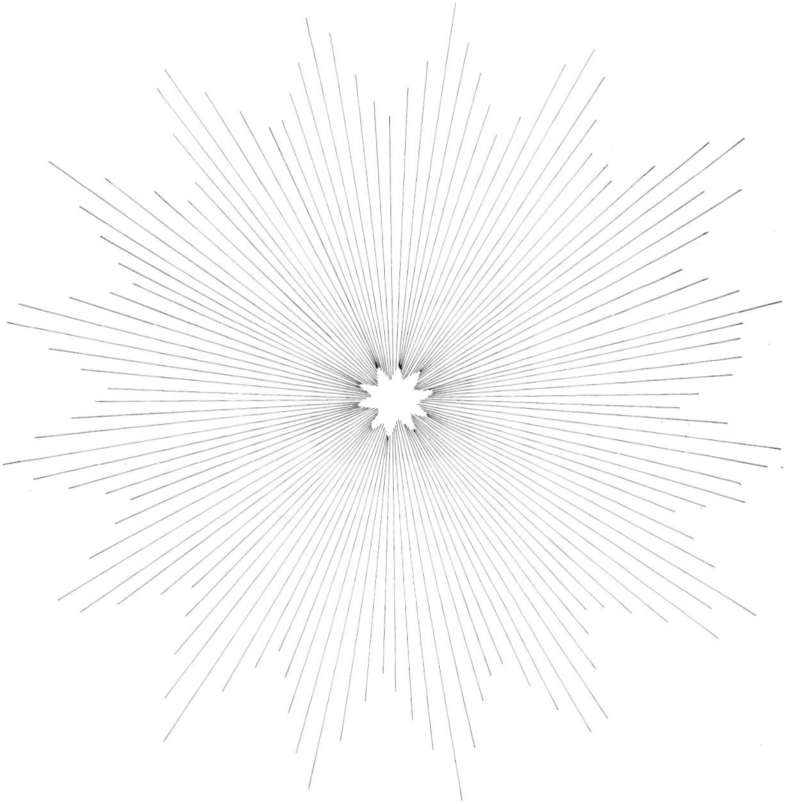

The Third Day

1. First arrange an altar with offerings for the Buddhas and Bodhisattvas.

2. Recite three to seven times The Invocation Prayer requesting blessings for their assistance and protection from the dangers of the bardo.

3. Recite The Liberation Through Hearing Mantra seven or 21 or 108 times:

A BI JA DAN GA

4. Call the name of the dying person three to seven times, and recite the instruction many times.

"XXX, Listen very carefully.

"Today the Buddha Ratna-Sambhava from the Southern pure realm manifests. Yellow in color, he holds a jewel in his hand. He sits on a horse-throne and embraces his consort Sangay-Chanma. He is also accompanied by two Bodhisattvas, Akasha-Garbha and Samantha-Bhadra, and two female attendants, Mala and Dhupa.

"A dazzling yellow light shines out from the heart of Buddha Ratna-Sambhava and his consort, and penetrates your heart. This light is so bright that your eyes can hardly bear to look at it.

"Along with it, a dull bluish-yellow light from the human realm also shines upon your heart. Due to the influence of pride and ego, you may turn away from the dazzling yellow light and wish to flee from it.

"Instead, you will feel more comfortable with the dull bluish-yellow light from the human realm. At this critical time you must ignore the dull bluish-yellow light. If you are drawn to it, you will fall into the human world where you will continue to face the misery of birth, old age, sickness, and death as well as continuing the cycle of reincarnation without end.

"Just focus your whole attention on the dazzling bright yellow light with total faith and devotion and pray:

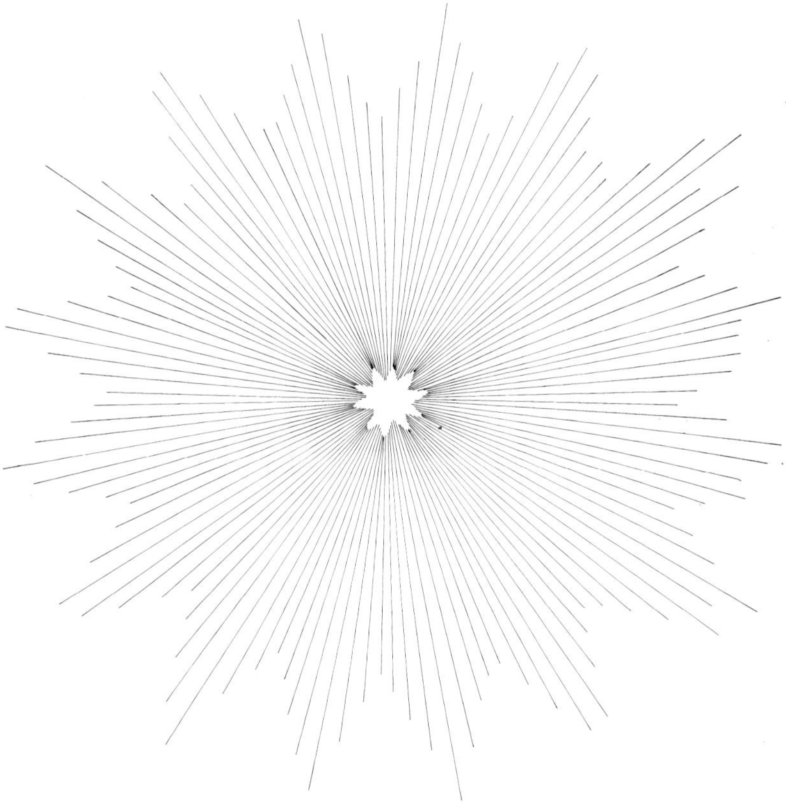

"Due to the influence of intense pride and ego,
I wander through the cycle of birth and death.
May the Buddha Ratna-Sambhava lead the way,
Consort Sangay-Chanma guard me from behind,
Escort me through the dangerous narrow path of the bardo
And lead me to the state of perfect enlightenment.

"Now put your trust and faith in the dazzling radiant yellow light, and dissolve yourself into the heart of Buddha Ratna-Sambhava. You will transcend the cycle of reincarnation and attain liberation."

The Fourth Day

1. First arrange an altar with offerings for the Buddhas and Bodhisattvas.

2. Recite three to seven times The Invocation Prayer requesting blessings for their assistance and protection from the dangers of the bardo.

3. Recite The Liberation Through Hearing Mantra seven or 21 or 108 times:

A BI JA DAN GA

4. Call the name of the dying person three to seven times, and recite the instruction many times.

"XXX, Listen very carefully.

"On this fourth day the Buddha Amitabha from the Western Pure Land appears before you. He is red in color and holds a lotus in his hand. He sits upon a peacock-throne and embraces his consort Pandaravasini. He is accompanied by two Bodhisattvas, Avalokitesvara and Manjushri, and two female attendants, Gita and Aloka.

"From the heart of Buddha Amitabha and his consort emits a dazzling radiant bright light that penetrates your heart. The light is so brilliant that your eyes will hardly be able to look at it.

"Along with it appears a dull red light from the hungry ghost realm which also shines upon you. Due to the influence of avarice and miserliness you will be afraid of the brilliant light. Instead you may feel more comfortable with the dull red light from the hungry ghost realms.

"If you follow the dull red light, you'll fall into the realm of hungry ghosts, and will endure unbearable sufferings of hunger and thirst. Don't look at it. Look at the brilliant red radiance and offer the following prayer wholeheartedly:

"Due to desire and attachment I wander through the cycle of existence.
May Buddha Amitabha lead the way,
Consort Pandaravasini guard me from behind,

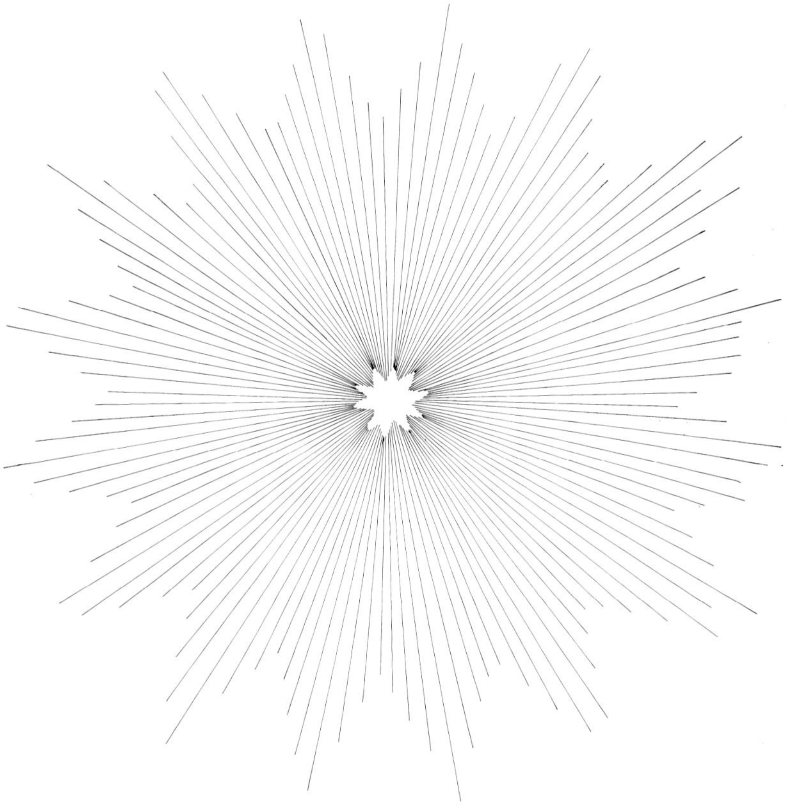

Guide me through the dangerous narrow path of the bardo
And lead me to the ground of perfect enlightenment.

"Now melt yourself into the dazzling rainbow light. Then you will transcend the cycle of birth and death and attain liberation."

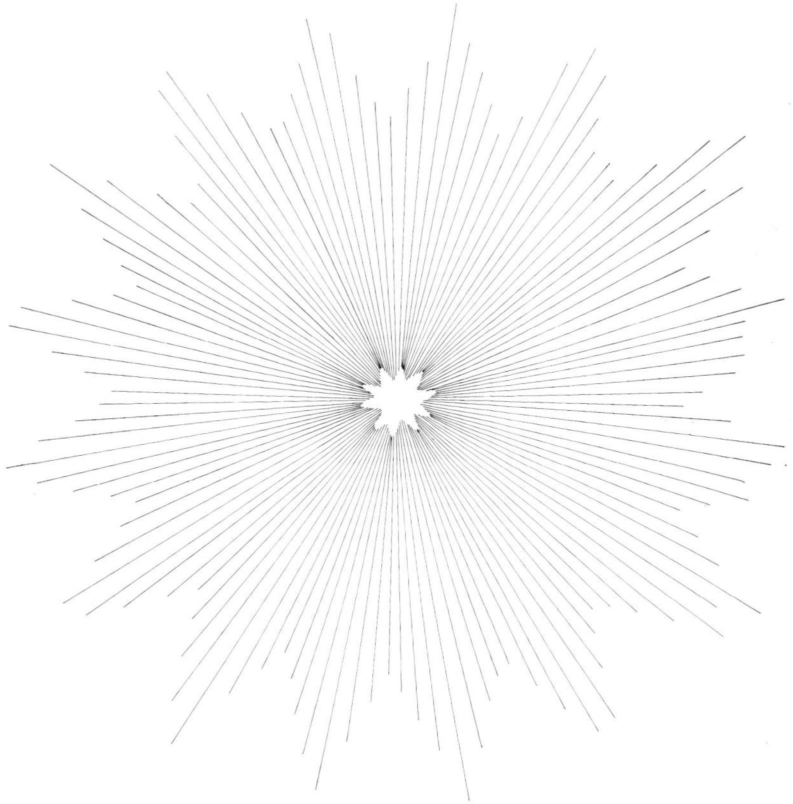

The Fifth Day

1. First arrange an altar with offerings for the Buddhas and Bodhisattvas.

2. Recite three to seven times The Invocation Prayer requesting blessings for their assistance and protection from the dangers of the bardo.

3. Recite The Liberation Through Hearing Mantra seven or 21 or 108 times:

A BI JA DAN GA

4. Call the name of the dying person three to seven times, and recite the instruction many times.

"XXX, Listen very carefully.

"On this fifth day, the Buddha Amogga-Siddi is coming from the Northern realm and appears before you. He is green in color and holds a crossed-vajra in his hand, and is in union with his consort Samaya-Tara. He sits upon an eagle throne, and is accompanied by two male Bodhisattvas, Vajrapani and Sarvanivarana-Viskambhin and two female attendants, Gandha and Naivedya.

"From the heart of the Buddha Amogha-Siddi and his consort emits a dazzling and radiant light directly at your heart. It is so bright that you will hardly be able to look at it. Due to the influence of jealousy, you will fear the dazzling radiant light and want to flee from it. At the same time a dull green light from the Assura (Titan) realm also shines upon you.

"Ignore the dull green light from the Assura realm. Don't even look at it. If you follow it you will fall into the Assura realm and endure endless conflicts and wars.

"Instead, you must not be intimidated by the brilliant green light. It is the radiance of the Buddha Amogga-Siddi and his consort coming to lead you through the path of bardo. Put your total trust in the brilliant light and offer whole-heartedly the following prayer:

> "Driven by jealousy I wander through the wheel of incarnation.
> May the Buddha Amogga-Siddi lead the way,
> Consort Samaya-Tara guard me from behind,

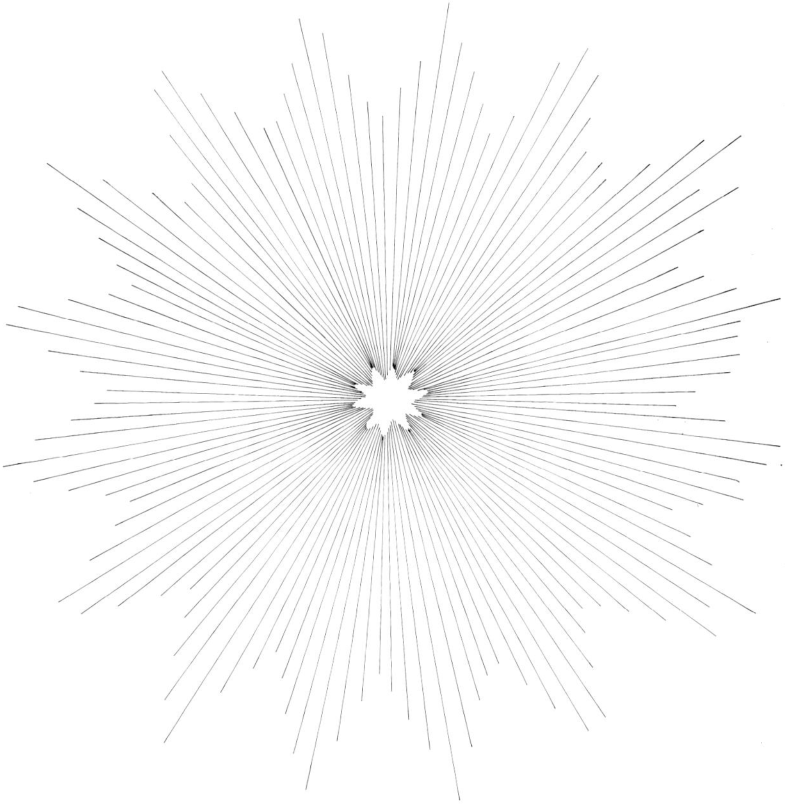

Guide me through the dangerous narrow path of the bardo,
And lead me to the ground of perfect enlightenment.

"Now recognize and melt into the brilliant rainbow light into the heart of Buddha Amogga-Siddi. Then you will transcend the wheel of incarnation and reach liberation."

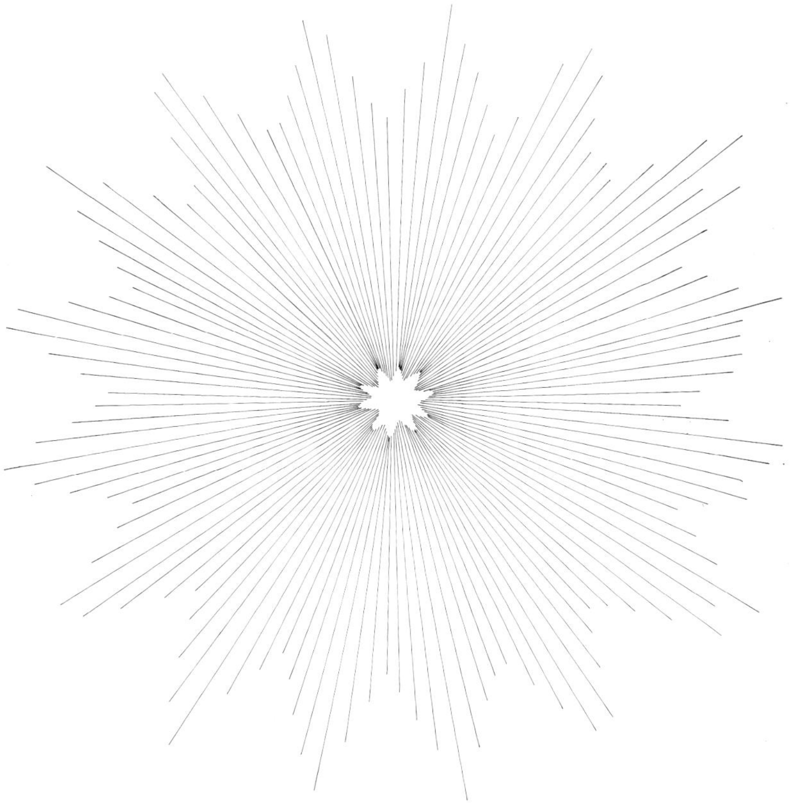

The Sixth Day

1. First arrange an altar with offerings for the Buddhas and Bodhisattvas.

2. Recite three to seven times The Invocation Prayer requesting blessings for their assistance and protection from the dangers of the bardo.

3. Recite The Liberation Through Hearing Mantra seven or 21 or 108 times:

A BI JA DAN GA

4. Call the name of the dying person three to seven times, and recite the instruction many times.

"XXX, Listen very carefully.

"Over the past five days the radiances of the five Buddhas have appeared to you. However, owing to the influence of your negative karma you were not able to recognize any one of them and still remain here. If you had recognized one of those radiances which emanated from your own essential nature, you would have attained liberation through merging into one or another of the five Buddhas.

"On this sixth day, all five Buddhas and their consorts and attendants are coming simultaneously to escort you at this precarious time.

"Buddha Variochana and his consort and retinue appear in the Center.
Buddha Vajra-Sattva with his consort and retinue appear in the East.
Buddha Ratna-Sambhava with his consort and retinue appear in the South.
Buddha Amitabha with his consort and retinue appear in the West.
Buddha Amogga-Siddi with his consort and retinue appear in the North.

"Each of the five Buddhas embrace their consorts, and each group is encircled with rainbow light.

"From the hearts of each of these five Buddhas and their consorts emit the extreme pure lights of the four wisdoms. Together they shine like a ribbon of sunbeams in your heart.

"From the heart of Buddha Variochana emits the radiant blue light.
From the heart of Buddha Amogga-Siddi emits the radiant green light.
From the heart of Buddha Ratna-Sambhava emits the radiant yellow light.
From the heart of Buddha Amitabha emits the radiant red light.
From the heart of Vajra-Sattva emits the radiant white light.

"At the same time the impure delusive lights of the six realms also appear:

"The dull white light of devas;
The dull green light of Assuras;
The dull yellow light of humans;
The dull blue light of animals;
The dull reddish light of hungry ghosts; and
The gray smoke-colored light of Hell.

"Be alert! Don't be drawn into any of these dull lights. Otherwise, you will be reborn into one of these impure existences and remain in the cycle of perpetual birth and death.

"Now pray wholeheartedly:

"Driven by the powerful forces of negative karma
I wander through the cycle of endless incarnation.
May the five Buddhas lead the way,
The five Consorts guard me from behind,
Lead me through the dangerous narrow path of the bardo,
And show me the way to the state of perfect enlightenment.

"Now you must focus your whole attention on the brilliant dazzling pure lights without fear, and melt into them. You will instantly transcend the cycle of existence and attain liberation."

The Seventh Day

1. First arrange an altar with offerings for the Buddhas and Bodhisattvas.

2. Recite three to seven times The Invocation Prayer requesting blessings for their assistance and protection from the dangers of the bardo.

3. Recite The Liberation Through Hearing Mantra seven or 21 or 108 times:

A BI JA DAN GA

4. Call the name of the dying person three to seven times, and recite the instruction many times.

"XXX, Listen very carefully.

"On this seventh day, the multi-colored radiance of the purified negativity comes to shine simultaneously. Also the knowledge-holders from the pure lands come to rescue you.

"From the center of the mandala, enveloped in a radiance of rainbow light, is the supreme knowledge-holder, known as The Lord of the Dance. He is embraced by his red dakini, radiating all the five colors of lights.

"In the East of the mandala, comes the earth-abiding knowledge-holder. White in color, with a radiant smiling countenance, he is embraced by his white dakini.

"In the South of the mandala, comes the longevity knowledge-holder. Yellow in color, smiling and radiant, he is embraced by his yellow dakini.

"In the West of the mandala comes the great symbol knowledge-holder. Red in color, smiling and radiant, he is embraced by his red dakini.

"In the North of the mandala, comes the self-involved knowledge-holder. Green in color, half smiling, half angry, he is embraced by his green dakini.

"Outside of the mandala, all around the knowledge-holders, are countless groups of dakinis from all places. Each knowledge-holder carries a bloody knife and a blood-filled skull

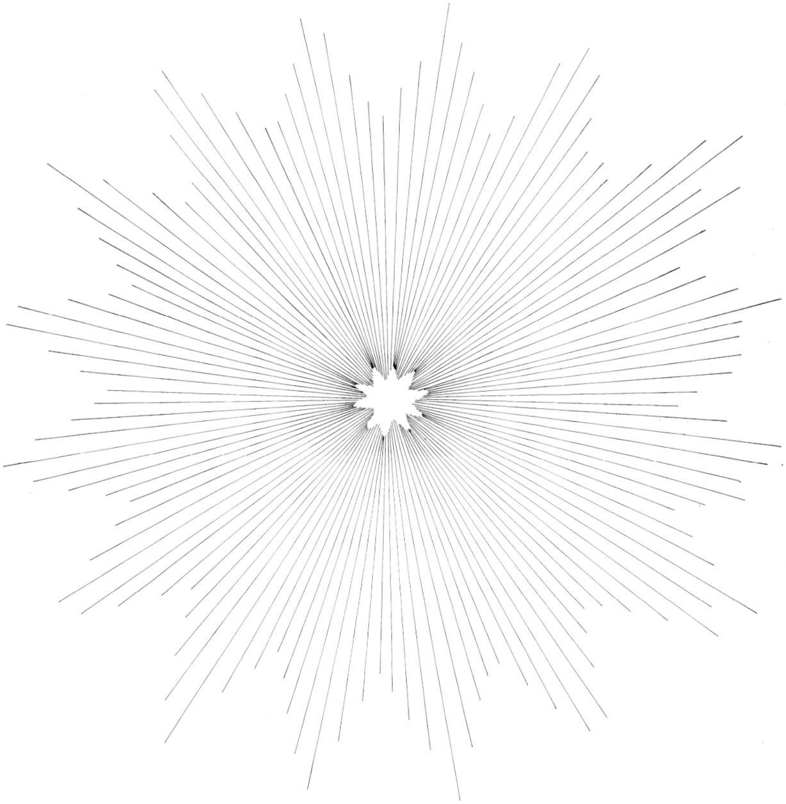

cup and looks at the sky. From the hearts of the five knowledge-holders comes forth five-colored radiances of wisdom, dazzling and flashing, that penetrates right into your heart.

"The lights are so bright that the eyes can barely look at them. At the same time, a dull blue light from the animal world also comes to shine upon you. Due to your heavy karmic influence, you will be afraid of the five-colored brilliant radiance. You will want to flee from them. Instead, you will feel more comfortable with the dull blue light from the animal world. Ignore the dull blue light. Don't even look at it. If you are lured by it and follow it, you will fall into the animal world and you will suffer the miseries of slavery, ignorance, and stupidity.

"Don't be intimidated by the dazzling five-colored radiance from the knowledge-holders and their dakinis. Pray earnestly for their assistance:

> "Driven by the powerful force of negative karma,
> I wander through the cycle of birth and death.
> May the knowledge-holders lead the way,
> The dakini consorts guard me from behind,
> Help me go through the dangerous, narrow path of the bardo
> And lead me to perfect enlightenment.

"Now merge yourself into the radiance from the hearts of the knowledge-holders and dakinis. You will transcend the cycle of existence and attain liberation instantly."

PHASE II

Now people will enter the second phase of the seven days, starting from Day Eight to Day Fourteen. At this time the situation is less favorable because the mind of the dying person is more fearful and less aware. In addition the Buddhas now appear in the form of fearful deities.

The Eighth Day

1. First arrange an altar with offerings for the Buddhas and Bodhisattvas.

2. Recite three to seven times The Invocation Prayer requesting blessings for their assistance and protection from the dangers of the bardo.

3. Recite The Liberation Through Hearing Mantra seven or 21 or 108 times:

A BI JA DAN GA

4. Call the name of the dying person three to seven times, and recite the instruction many times.

"XXX, Listen very carefully.

"During the previous seven days, the five Buddhas and their entourages manifested peacefully before you. But you were not able to recognize them. Hence, you are still wandering here.

"On this eighth day the wrathful deity, the great, glorious Buddha-Heruka comes before you.

"Buddha-Heruka is dark brown in color, with three heads, six hands and four legs. He has three faces, and each face has three eyes. His right face is white, his left face is red, and his middle face is dark brown. He is embraced by his consort Buddha Krotishaurima. Great thunder sounds, and great flames of radiance emit from their bodies.

"Don't be frightened by their appearances. They are actually the changed forms of Buddha Variochana and his consort, The Lady of the Space.

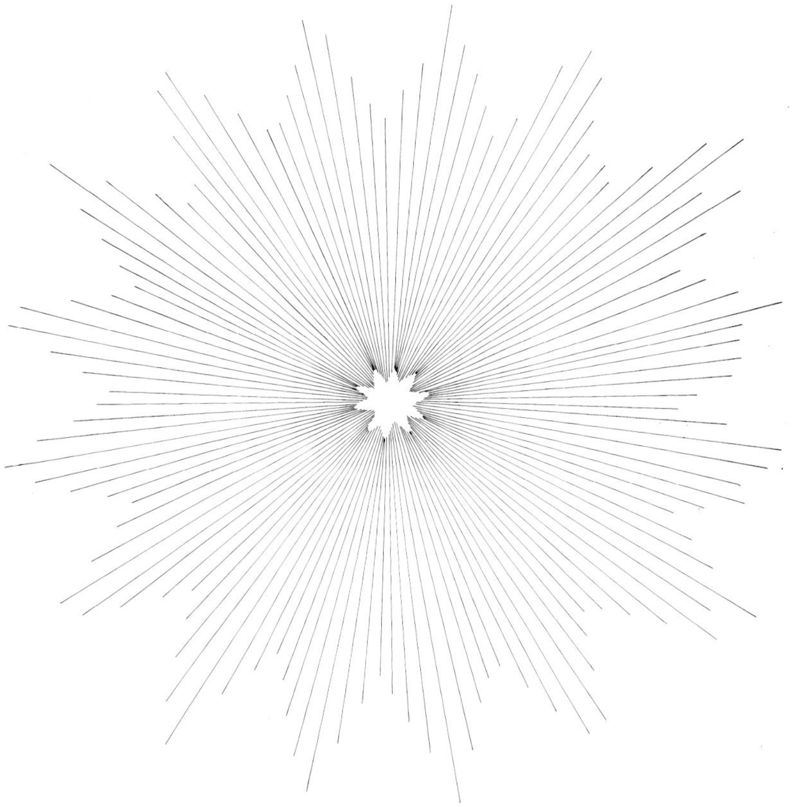

They are also the reflections of your inner mind.

"Recognize them and melt into them.

"You will be liberated instantly."

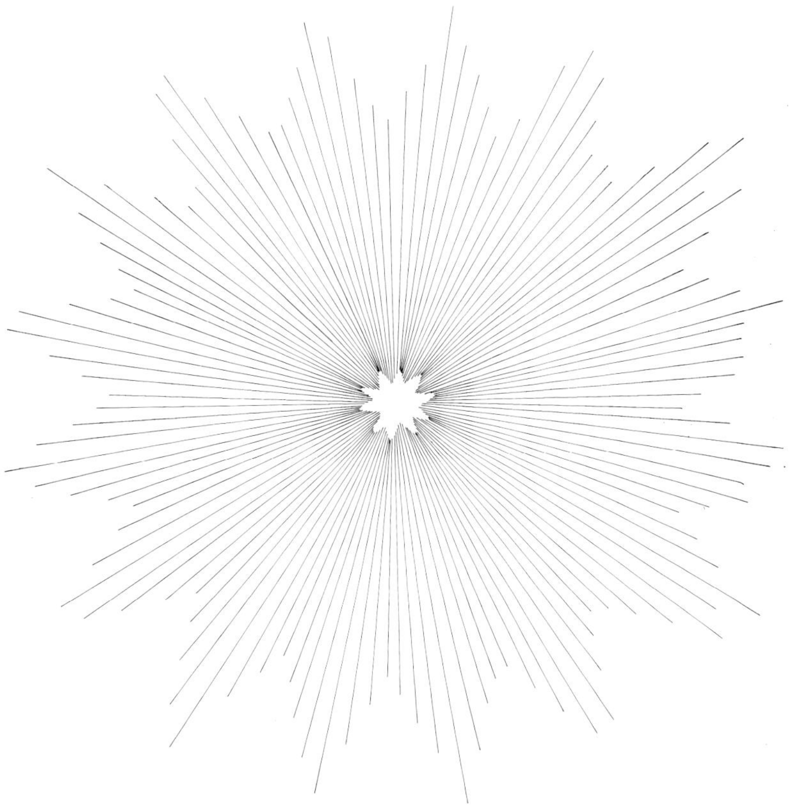

The Ninth Day

1. First arrange an altar with offerings for the Buddhas and Bodhisattvas.

2. Recite three to seven times The Invocation Prayer requesting blessings for their assistance and protection from the dangers of the bardo.

3. Recite The Liberation Through Hearing Mantra seven or 21 or 108 times:

A BI JA DAN GA

4. Call the name of the dying person three to seven times, and recite the instruction many times.

"XXX, Listen very carefully.

"On this ninth day, the blood-drinking deity Vajra-Heruka and his entourage appear from the East before you. He is dark blue in color, with three faces. Each face has three eyes, six hands and four legs. His right face is white, his left face is red and his middle face is dark-blue. He is embraced by his consort Vajra-Krotishaurima.

"Don't be frightened! These deities are the changed forms of Buddha Vajra-Sattva and his consort. The images are the reflections of your inner mind.

"Believe them and recognize them.

"Merge into them.

"You will be liberated instantly."

The Tenth Day

1. First arrange an altar with offerings for the Buddhas and Bodhisattvas.

2. Recite three to seven times The Invocation Prayer requesting blessings for their assistance and protection from the dangers of the bardo.

3. Recite The Liberation Through Hearing Mantra seven or 21 or 108 times:

A BI JA DAN GA

4. Call the name of the dying person three to seven times, and recite the instruction many times.

"XXX, Listen very carefully.

"On this tenth day Ratna-Heruka and his entourage in wrathful appearance emerges from the South before you. He is yellow in color with three faces. Each face has three eyes, six hands and four legs. His right face is white, his left face is red, and his middle face is dark yellow. He is embraced by his consort Ratna-Krotishaurima.

"Don't be frightened by their appearances. They are in fact the reflections of your own inner mind, and they are the changed forms of Buddha Ratna-Sambhava and his consort.

"Recognize them as such and melt into them.

"You will be liberated instantly."

The Eleventh Day

1. First arrange an altar with offerings for the Buddhas and Bodhisattvas.

2. Recite three to seven times The Invocation Prayer requesting blessings for their assistance and protection from the dangers of the bardo.

3. Recite The Liberation Through Hearing Mantra seven or 21 or 108 times:

A BI JA DAN GA

4. Call the name of the dying person three to seven times, and recite the instruction many times.

"XXX, Listen very carefully.

"On this eleventh day, the blood-drinking Padma-Heruka and his retinue appears from the West before you. He is reddish-black in color with three faces, each with three eyes. The right face is white, the left blue, and the middle is dark red. He has six hands and four legs, and he is embraced by his consort Padma-Krotishaurima.

"Don't be afraid! Rejoice! These are the reflections of your inner self, and the changed forms of Buddha Amitabha and his consort.

"Trust them and recognize them.

"Merge into them.

"You will be liberated instantly!"

The Twelfth Day

1. First arrange an altar with offerings for the Buddhas and Bodhisattvas.

2. Recite three to seven times The Invocation Prayer requesting blessings for their assistance and protection from the dangers of the bardo.

3. Recite The Liberation Through Hearing Mantra seven or 21 or 108 times:

A BI JA DAN GA

4. Call the name of the dying person three to seven times, and recite the instruction many times.

"XXX, Listen very carefully.

"On this twelfth day, the blood-drinking deity Kama-Heruka with his consort, and accompanied by Kerima, Ittamenina, and Wang Chugma appear from the North before you. Kama-Heruka is dark green in color with three faces, each with three eyes. His right face is white, his left face is red, and his middle face is dark green. He has six hands and four legs, and he is embraced by his consort Kama-Krotishaurima.

"Don't be terrified! These deities are the reflection of your inner mind, and the changed manifestations of Buddha Amogga-Siddi and his consort.

"Recognize them and merge into them.

"You will be liberated instantly!"

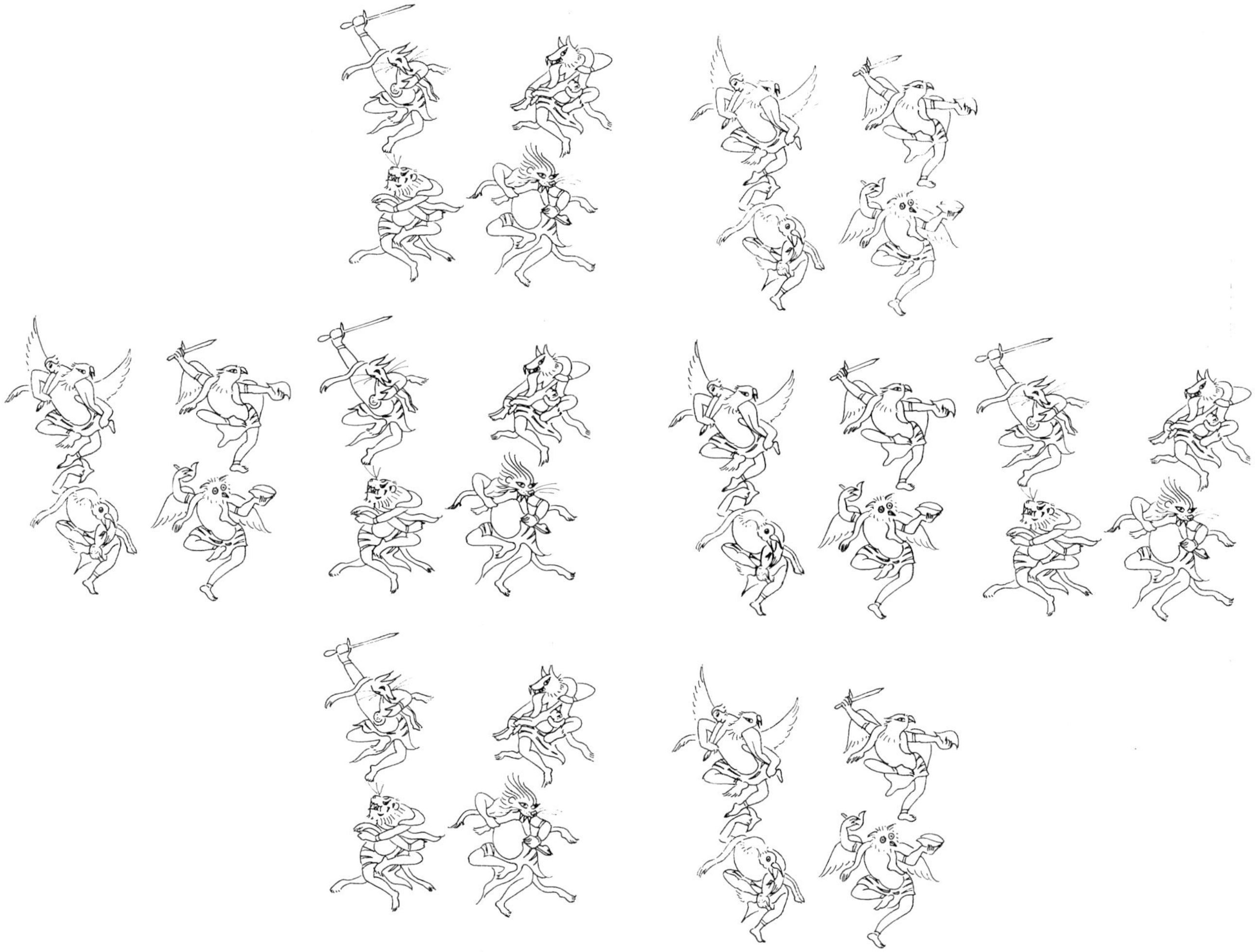

The Thirteenth Day

1. First arrange an altar with offerings for the Buddhas and Bodhisattvas.

2. Recite three to seven times The Invocation Prayer requesting blessings for their assistance and protection from the dangers of the bardo.

3. Recite The Liberation Through Hearing Mantra seven or 21 or 108 times:

A BI JA DAN GA

4. Call the name of the dying person three to seven times, and recite the instruction many times.

"XXX, Listen very carefully.

"On the thirteenth day of the Reality Stage, (the second stage), all five wrathful deities with their consorts and entourages come from eight directions to receive you.

"From the East, White Kerima.
From the South, Yellow Tsearima.
From the West, Red Bramha.
From the North, Black Petali.
From the Southeast, Red Pukkase.
From the Southwest, Dark Green Ghasmari.
From the Northwest, Yellow Tsandhali.
From the Northeast, Dark Blue Simasha.

"In addition, from the outside of the mandala come eight dakinis from eight directions. They are,

"From the East, Dark-Brown-Lion-Head.
From the South, Red-Tiger-Head.
From the West, Black-Fox-Head.
From the North, Dark-Blue-Wolf-Head.
From the Southeast, Yellow-White-Vulture-Head.

From the Southwest, Dark-Red-Cemetery-Bird-Head.
From the Northwest, Black-Crow-Head.
From the Northeast, Owl-Head.

"They surround the five blood-drinking deities.

"Don't be intimidated by them. They are the reflection of your primordial self and also the changed manifestations of the five Buddhas.

"Recognize them as such, and dissolve into them.

"You will be liberated instantly!"

The Fourteenth Day

1. First arrange an altar with offerings for the Buddhas and Bodhisattvas.

2. Recite three to seven times The Invocation Prayer requesting blessings for their assistance and protection from the dangers of the bardo.

3. Recite The Liberation Through Hearing Mantra seven or 21 or 108 times:

A BI JA DAN GA

4. Call the name of the dying person three to seven times, and recite the instruction many times.

"XXX, Listen very carefully.

"Today is the fourteenth day of the Reality Stage of the Bardo, the last day of this stage. It is the final opportunity to attain liberation. If you fail, you may fall into the miserable worlds of suffering.

"Four female door-keepers appear before you:

> "From the East, the white tiger-headed goddess holding a goad.
> From the South, the yellow-sow-headed goddess holding a noose.
> From the West, the red-lion-headed goddess holding an iron chain.
> From the North, the green serpent-headed goddess holding a bell.

"On the outside area of the mandala, there are thirty wrathful deities and twenty-eight various-headed mighty goddesses, holding various weapons. They also come before you.

"Don't be frightened. Think that they are your protectors that have come to guide you through the dangerous path of the bardo. Then pray whole-heartedly:

> "Driven by the powerful forces of negative karma,
> I wander through the cycle of birth and death.
> May the peaceful and wrathful deities lead the way,

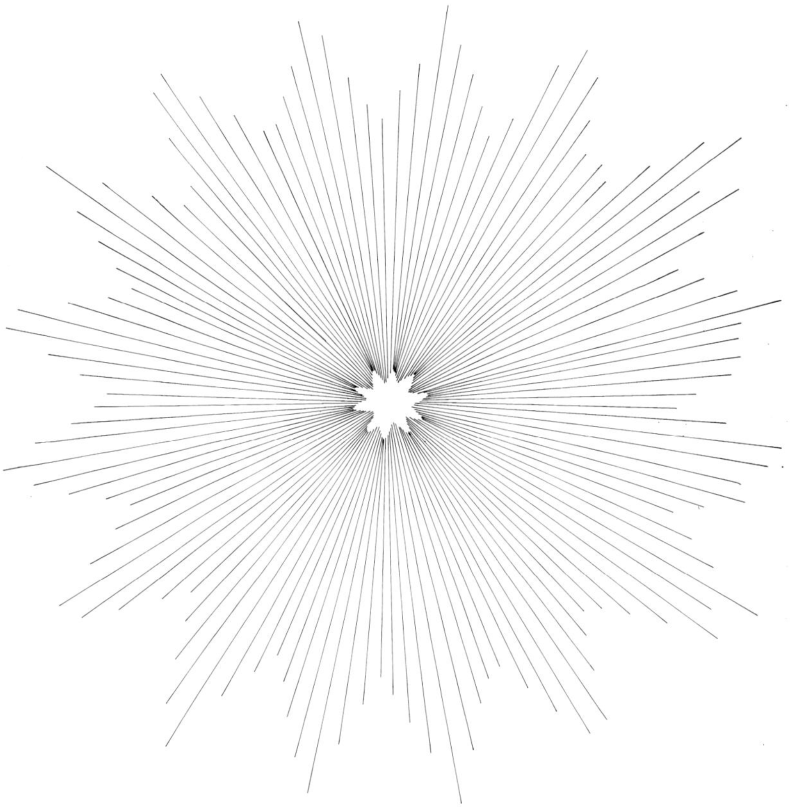

The blessed goddesses guard me from behind,
And save me from the fearful narrow path of the bardo
And put me in the state of perfect enlightenment.

"Now all these deities and goddesses emit a radiance that shines upon you. You should know that all these are the reflections of your primordial mind.

"Recognize them as such and merge into them.

"You will be liberated instantly!"

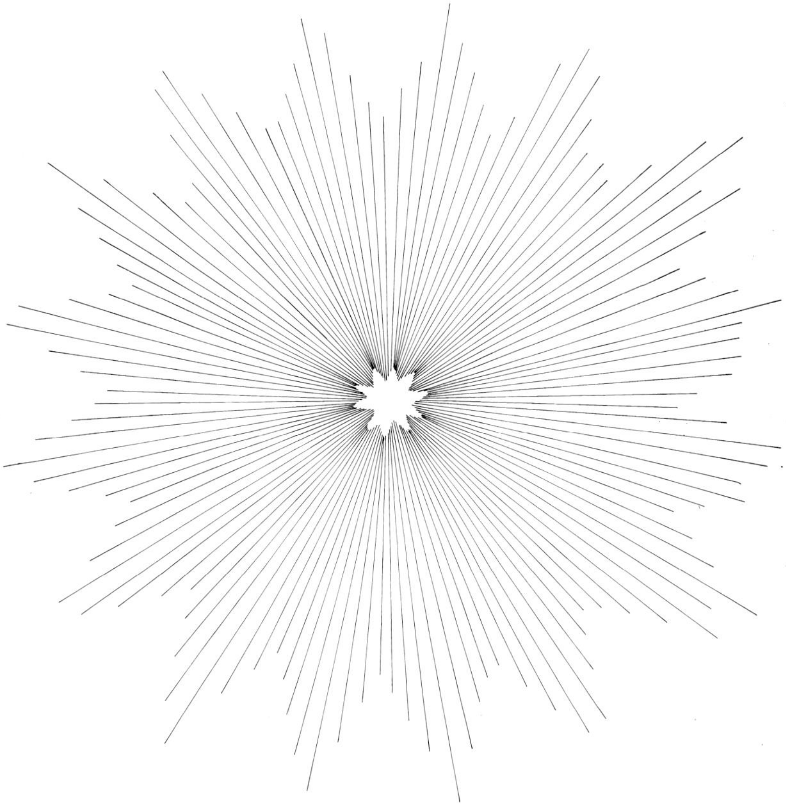

THE THIRD STAGE – BECOMING

After the experience of fourteen days and multiple times of instruction to the deceased, due to the heavy influence of negative karma, still he/she has not been able to recognize The Clear Light. Now the deceased sinks into this period of reincarnation. The condition in this period is less favorable. However, even in this late stage, there are opportunities for the deceased to attain liberation. The primary activities are:

1. How to close the door of a bad womb, and

2. How to choose an auspicious womb for rebirth.

The Natural State of Mind

1. First arrange an altar with offerings for the Buddhas and Bodhisattvas.

2. Recite three to seven times The Invocation Prayer requesting blessings for their assistance and protection from the dangers of the bardo.

3. Recite The Liberation Through Hearing Mantra seven or 21 or 108 times:

A BI JA DAN GA

4. Call the name of the dying person three to seven times, and recite the instruction many times.

"XXX, Listen carefully.

"For the last fourteen days you have experienced the appearances of the Peaceful and Wrathful Buddha forms who came to receive you. Due to fear and the influence of negative karma, you failed to recognize them. Now you have wandered down this far on the bardo path.

"At this time you may be able to see or sense your future rebirth.

"If you are to be born as a deva, the deva realm will appear to you. The same applies to the other five realms. Be alert! Don't follow the negative and wrathful visions. Otherwise, you will have to wander into the cycle of perpetual birth and death. Instead, rest your mind in the natural state of nothing-to-do and nothing-to-hold condition.

"You will be liberated!"

The State of Non-Attachment

1. First arrange an altar with offerings for the Buddhas and Bodhisattvas.

2. Recite three to seven times The Invocation Prayer requesting blessings for their assistance and protection from the dangers of the bardo.

3. Recite The Liberation Through Hearing Mantra seven or 21 or 108 times:

A BI JA DAN GA

4. Call the name of the dying person three to seven times, and recite the instruction many times.

"XXX, Listen carefully.

"You are now in the Incarnation Bardo Period. You may feel a moment of great joy followed by a moment of deep sorrow. Don't attach yourself to these feelings.

"At the same time, if you are to be born in a certain realm, the vision of that realm will be drawn toward you.

"Don't attach yourself to any worldly things that you have left behind. Don't worry about whoever takes possession of them and uses them. Don't feel angry. If you get angry, even though you are supposed to be born into a higher and happier realm, you will wind up in a lower realm. Therefore, renounce worldly things, and instead think that you are offering them to the Precious Trinity and your Guru. Above all, abide in the state of non-attachment. You will be liberated."

Staying Calm in the Face of Terrors

1. First arrange an altar with offerings for the Buddhas and Bodhisattvas.

2. Recite three to seven times The Invocation Prayer requesting blessings for their assistance and protection from the dangers of the bardo.

3. Recite The Liberation Through Hearing Mantra seven or 21 or 108 times:

A BI JA DAN GA

4. Call the name of the dying person three to seven times, and recite the instruction many times.

"XXX, Listen carefully.

"Now you are in the Third Stage of the Incarnation of the Bardo. You can see your relatives, friends and loved ones, and even your own corpse. You can see your family weeping. You know that you are dead. These visions cause you great fear and anguish.

"All around you, day and night, is a gray twilight-like light. You will remain in this state for about twenty to thirty-five days, depending upon your karmic influence.

"During this time you will experience many terrors, such as the sounds of mountains crashing down all around you; lakes and rivers flooding; great fires, windstorms; snow and hail whirling all around you. You will feel that you are being chased by humans, demons, and wild beasts to the brink of three precipices; one white, one red, and one black. You will also feel that you are being squeezed into the cracks and crevices of boulders and rocks. All this is the mental projection of your inner mind. Once you renounce greed, anger, and ignorance all three precipices will disappear.

"Now you have an urge to acquire a body. At this critical moment you can easily go up or fall down on the ladder of rebirth. Stop the desire to have a body. Instead, visualize that The Lord of Compassion appears before you, and pray earnestly for his assistance, and then dissolve into the radiant void. You will achieve liberation."

Judgment

1. First arrange an altar with offerings for the Buddhas and Bodhisattvas.

2. Recite three to seven times The Invocation Prayer requesting blessings for their assistance and protection from the dangers of the bardo.

3. Recite The Liberation Through Hearing Mantra seven or 21 or 108 times:

A BI JA DAN GA

4. Call the name of the dying person three to seven times, and recite the instruction many times.

"XXX, Listen carefully.

"The suffering you are experiencing is the result of your own negative actions in the past. Don't blame anybody. Pray to the Precious Trinity and The Lord of Compassion and to your Guru for their protection. The Lord of Death will come to count out and weigh your good deeds with white pebbles, and will come to count out and weigh the evil deeds you have committed in the past with black pebbles.

"You will be very frightened and will attempt to rationalize or lie about your bad deeds. The Lord of Death will look into the mirror of karma which reflects every good and evil deed you have committed. If you lie, an executioner will drag you into Hell, and severely torture your body.

"Therefore, don't lie! Be aware. Since your current body is a mental body and cannot be killed even through beheading, there is no reason to fear.

"All these images are only the illusory reflections of your past karma."

Abide in the Natural Primordial State

1. First arrange an altar with offerings for the Buddhas and Bodhisattvas.

2. Recite three to seven times The Invocation Prayer requesting blessings for their assistance and protection from the dangers of the bardo.

3. Recite The Liberation Through Hearing Mantra seven or 21 or 108 times:

A BI JA DAN GA

4. Call the name of the dying person three to seven times, and recite the instruction many times.

"XXX, Listen Carefully.

"At this time, the memory of the past body will gradually fade away while the appearance of the future body becomes clearer. You are anxiously searching for a body wherein you are to be reborn. Depending upon the karmic influence, the most compatible body for you will shine most prominently.

"The following are the lights of the six realms:

"A dull white light from the Deva world.
A dull green light from the Assura world.
A dull yellow light from the Human world.
A dull blue light from the Animal world.
A dull red light from the Hungry Ghost world.
A dull gray smoke-colored light from Hell.

"At this time, by the power of karma, your mental body will take on the same color of the realm into which you will be born. It is critically important that regardless of which color light shines before you, and no matter how alluring they are, that you don't follow anyone

of them. Instead, meditate and turn your mind on The Lord of Compassion and abide in the natural primordial state.

"You will be liberated from the cycle of birth and death!"

Closing the Womb Doors

Abandon Negative Passions

1. First arrange an altar with offerings for the Buddhas and Bodhisattvas.

2. Recite three to seven times The Invocation Prayer requesting blessings for their assistance and protection from the dangers of the bardo.

3. Recite The Liberation Through Hearing Mantra seven or 21 or 108 times:

A BI JA DAN GA

4. Call the name of the dying person three to seven times, and recite the instruction many times.

"XXX, Listen carefully.

"This is the critical moment of decision between going up or falling down. Make a resolution not to harbor any evil thoughts or evil acts. If you enter a womb from the forces of negative passions, you will be reborn as a human, or an animal, or a hungry ghost, or even into Hell. Therefore, it is extremely important at this time to avoid any negative passions such as anger, desire, ego, greed, ignorance, or jealousy. They are the inner enemies which have caused you to fall into the ocean of misery. Meditate this way whole-heartedly. Then the door to rebirth in an inappropriate womb will be closed."

Beseech Blessings and Guidance from Your Guru and Lord of Compassion

1. First arrange an altar with offerings for the Buddhas and Bodhisattvas.

2. Recite three to seven times The Invocation Prayer requesting blessings for their assistance and protection from the dangers of the bardo.

3. Recite The Liberation Through Hearing Mantra seven or 21 or 108 times:

A BI JA DAN GA

4. Call the name of the dying person three to seven times, and recite the instruction many times.

"XXX, Listen carefully.

"You will see visions of a male and a female in union. Even though you have the urge to join in, you must restrain yourself from going in between them. Instead, you should think that they are your Guru and his consort, or The Lord of Compassion and his consort. Respectfully make offerings to them in your mind and beseech their blessings and guidance. The door to the womb will be closed."

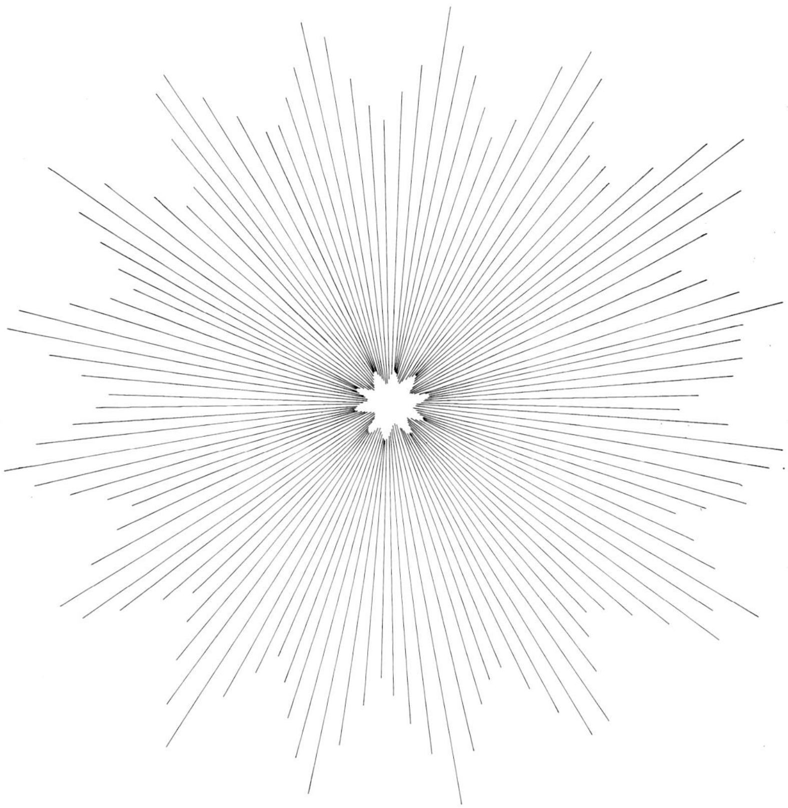

Abandon Attachments, Hatreds, and Revulsions

1. First arrange an altar with offerings for the Buddhas and Bodhisattvas.

2. Recite three to seven times The Invocation Prayer requesting blessings for their assistance and protection from the dangers of the bardo.

3. Recite The Liberation Through Hearing Mantra seven or 21 or 108 times:

A BI JA DAN GA

4. Call the name of the dying person three to seven times, and recite the instruction many times.

"XXX, Listen carefully.

"When the vision of a male and female in union appears before you, a feeling of jealousy will arise within you. If you are to be reborn as a male, you will feel desire for women and hatred for men. Conversely, if you are to be reborn as a female, you will feel desire for men and hatred for women. When these negative feelings happen, meditate as follows:

"Due to my heavy negative karma accumulated from beginningless time,
I have wandered in the cycle of perpetual birth and death,
Suffering in the ocean of misery.
Now I resolve to abandon all attachments and hatreds,
As well as the feelings of attraction and revulsion.

"If you can maintain this resolution whole-heartedly, the womb-door to rebirth will be automatically closed."

Meditate on the Illusion of All Images

1. First arrange an altar with offerings for the Buddhas and Bodhisattvas.

2. Recite three to seven times The Invocation Prayer requesting blessings for their assistance and protection from the dangers of the bardo.

3. Recite The Liberation Through Hearing Mantra seven or 21 or 108 times:

A BI JA DAN GA

4. Call the name of the dying person three to seven times, and recite the instruction many times.

"XXX, Listen carefully.

"Meditate that all images and scenes which have appeared to you are illusory without any substance. The male/female in union image is also illusory. All these images are like mirages, like visions in dreams, like the moon on the water. They are unreal. They are the hallucinations of your own mind. With this understanding, the entrance to the womb door will be blocked."

Meditate on The Clear Light

1. First arrange an altar with offerings for the Buddhas and Bodhisattvas.

2. Recite three to seven times The Invocation Prayer requesting blessings for their assistance and protection from the dangers of the bardo.

3. Recite The Liberation Through Hearing Mantra seven or 21 or 108 times:

A BI JA DAN GA

4. Call the name of the dying person three to seven times, and recite the instruction many times.

"XXX, Listen carefully.

"Meditate on The Clear Light. Visualize that all things are the reflection of your own mind and that your mind is not born, nor dying. Then rest your mind in the primordial state without any sense of duality, beyond all thoughts of good or bad, acceptance or rejection. Then the womb-doors to rebirth will be closed."

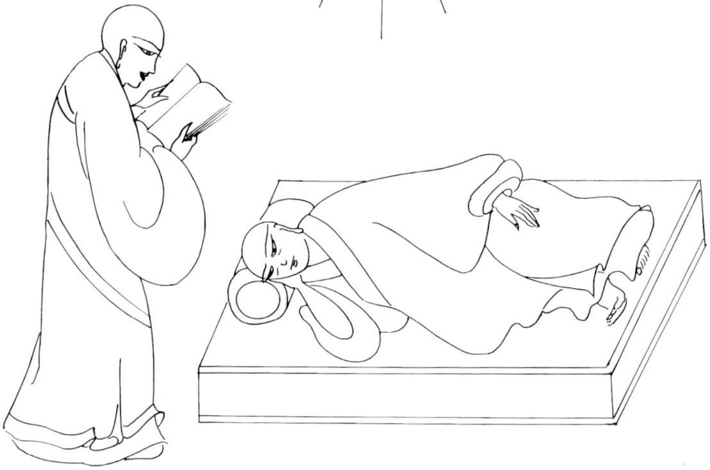

Choosing a Womb

Images of the Four Continents and Five Realms

1. First arrange an altar with offerings for the Buddhas and Bodhisattvas.

2. Recite three to seven times The Invocation Prayer requesting blessings for their assistance and protection from the dangers of the bardo.

3. Recite The Liberation Through Hearing Mantra seven or 21 or 108 times:

A BI JA DAN GA

4. Call the name of the dying person three to seven times, and recite the instruction many times.

"XXX, Listen carefully.

"Many ways to close the womb-door have been given to you. However, due to the influence of negative karma, you still have not been liberated. Now is the time to choose an appropriate and auspicious womb for you to take rebirth.

"First, the images of the Four Continents will appear to you.

> "1. The Eastern Continent of Lapah has beautiful lakes adorned with swans. It is prosperous but weak in spiritual teachings and practice. Therefore, do not choose to go there.
>
> 2. The Southern Continent of Jambu has grand mansions. This is the human world. If you want to be reborn as a human, you may enter this Continent.
>
> 3. The Western Continent of Balung-Chou has a lake surrounded with horses. Although this Continent has wealth and pleasures, it is weak in spiritual teachings and practices. Do not go there.
>
> 4. The Northern Continent of Daminyan has a lake surrounded with grazing cattle and trees. This is a land of good health and long life, but weak in spiritual teachings and practice. Do not go there."

"Second, the images of the Five Realms will appear to you.

"1. The Deva Realm has beautiful temples built with precious metals. It is an auspicious place. You may enter there.

2. The Assura Realm has beautiful forests and orchards and fire circles revolving in opposite directions. Do not enter there.

3. The Animal Realm has caves, tunnels, and deep holes in the earth. It appears dimly. Do not enter there.

4. The Hungry Ghost Realm has desolate plains with burned-out trees. The earth is dark, and the caves are deep and shallow. Do not enter there.

5. The Hell Realm has wailing cries, and is a land of gloom, with ugly red or black houses made of metal. Black holes cover the realm, and the roads are dark and dirty. Do not enter there.

"There are two ways to choose rebirth:

"1. Rebirth in a pure Buddha field.

2. Rebirth in an impure human world in order to continue spiritual practice."

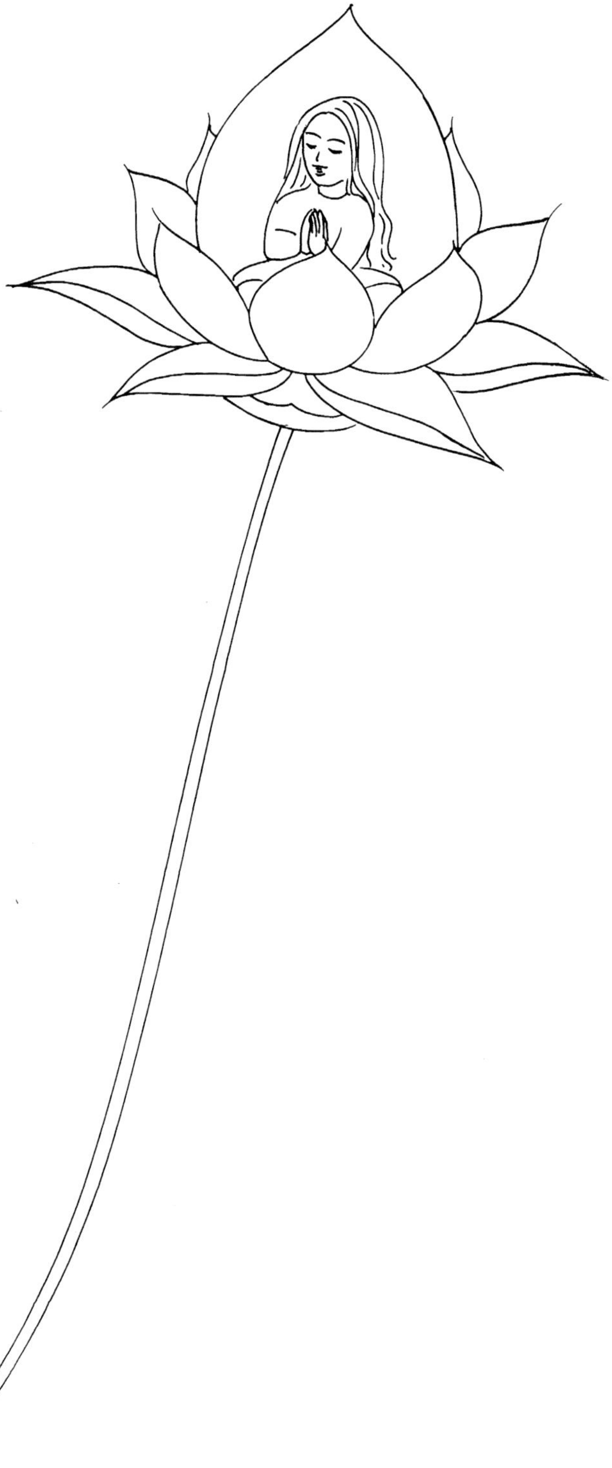

Amitabha Buddha's Pure Land or Auspicious Human Birth

1. First arrange an altar with offerings for the Buddhas and Bodhisattvas.

2. Recite three to seven times The Invocation Prayer requesting blessings for their assistance and protection from the dangers of the bardo.

3. Recite The Liberation Through Hearing Mantra seven or 21 or 108 times:

A BI JA DAN GA

4. Call the name of the dying person three to seven times, and recite the instruction many times.

"XXX, Listen carefully.

"1. Meditate that: it is most unfortunate that from beginningless time until now I have been wandering in the cycle of perpetual birth and death. I am exhausted and disgusted with this situation. I want no more of it. I resolve to take refuge in Buddha Amitabha and take rebirth in his Pure Land, in The Western Paradise.

"Hold onto this resolution firmly and you will instantly take rebirth in Buddha Amitabha's Western Paradise.

"2. Meditate that: I wish to take rebirth in the human world in order to be able to benefit others. I intend to choose to take rebirth in a body (or a family) endowed with great merits, in a nice place where spiritual teachings are flourishing.

"Hold onto this resolution firmly, and an appropriate and auspicious womb will appear before you. Then request the Buddhas and Bodhisattvas, particularly Bodhisattva Avalokitesvara, to bless the womb, transforming it into a divine abode. Then enter it and take rebirth. Before entering the womb you should resolve to devote your future life to spiritual practice for the benefit of all sentient beings.

"Be aware, for in choosing a womb it is possible to make a mistake. It is important to view the potential wombs in a spirit of detachment without grasping or aversion."

CONCLUSION

"The Great Liberation Through Hearing" offers many opportunities for people to achieve liberation during the transitional period of dying and death. The most superior practitioners who have had deep meditation experiences during their lifetimes need not go through the intermediate state, and will be able to liberate themselves at the moment of death. Hence, they bypass the transitional phase.

The lesser practitioners who have had some meditation experiences during their lifetimes may be able to attain liberation by recognizing The Clear Light which appears to them at the moment of death.

The ordinary people will be liberated through recognizing the various visions of the peaceful and wrathful deities and by merging into The Clear Light in the second bardo, during the following fourteen days, in accordance with their capacities and karmic influence.

For those with heavy negative karma, they have to wander downwards into the stage of becoming. However, even at that late stage there are opportunities for them to reach liberation by following instructions given to them.

Even the lowest ones still have opportunities to turn away from an unfavorable rebirth by closing the door of a bad womb and choosing an auspicious and appropriate womb for rebirth into a human body. This will enable them to live a virtual life and meet spiritual teachers for spiritual training and practice. Eventually they will attain liberation.

This great teaching serves as the catalyst which can lead to the state of liberation and enlightenment. It is like moving a heavy wooden log which one hundred men can't carry, but can be towed easily by floating in water.

Finally, it is important for one to study the teaching during one's lifetime and familiarize oneself with its contents. Let it sink deeply into ones heart to the extent that one would remember its words and meanings even if chased by seven wild dogs!

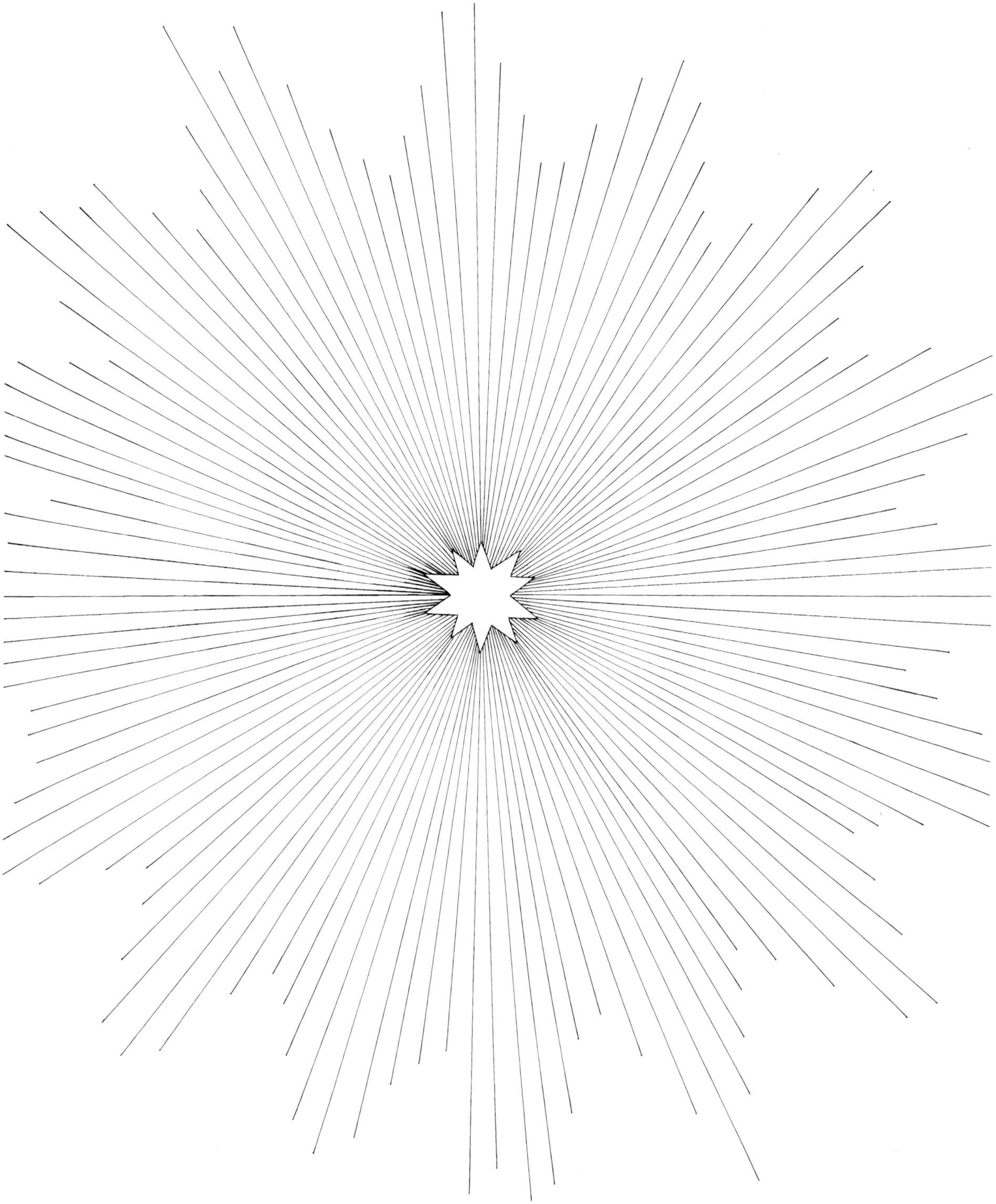

OM
MANI
PAD
ME
HUM

BIBLIOGRAPHY

1. W. Y. Evans-Wentz. *The Tibetan Book of the Dead* (Oxford University Press, 1927)

2. Yuen-Yin. *Tson-Yo (Bardo)* (Ho-Yu Publishing House: Tainan, Taiwan, 2006)

3. Glenn H. Mullin. *The Tibetan Book of the Dead* (Lustre Press/Roli Book, India, 2009)

4. Stephen Hodge with Martin Boord. *Tibetan Book of the Dead* (Sterling Publishing Company, Inc., N.Y. 1999)

5. Detlef Ingo Lauf. *Secret Doctrines of the Tibetan Book of the Dead* (Shambhala Publications Inc., 1989)

6. Chokyi Nyima Rinpoche. *The Bardo Guidebook* (Rangiung Yeshe Publications, Hong Kong, 1991)

Tze-si "Jesse" Huang is a professional writer and translator and native Chinese. He was born in Chungking, the youngest of ten children. After facing and overcoming the trials of both survival and becoming educated, recorded in his *Journey to the Unknown* (Fons Vitae, 2014), he eventually immigrated to the U.S.A. He attended New York University and Columbia University for post graduate studies. In 1975, he met his wife, the renowned children's book author and illustrator, Demi. In the United States he worked as a financial analyst and executive director in several companies while continuing to pursue his love of writing and translating from his native Chinese into English. His award winning title, *Master of Zen: Extraordinary Teachings from Hui Neng's Altar Sutra,* is an example of his excellent work. In 1990, both Tze-si Huang and his wife, Demi, represented the United States at the First Children's International Book Conference in Beijing.

Demi is an award-winning illustrator of numerous books for children, including biographies of spiritual figures such as Jesus, Muhammad, Buddha, the Dalai Lama, Saint Francis of Assisi, Lao Tzu, al-Ghazzali, and Joan of Arc. Her books include *The Empty Pot, The Nightingale, The Emperor's New Clothes*, and *Gandhi*, which was named the *New York Times* Best Illustrated Book and received the Oppenheim Toy Portfolio Platinum Award.